THE MAGIC OF PATIENCE

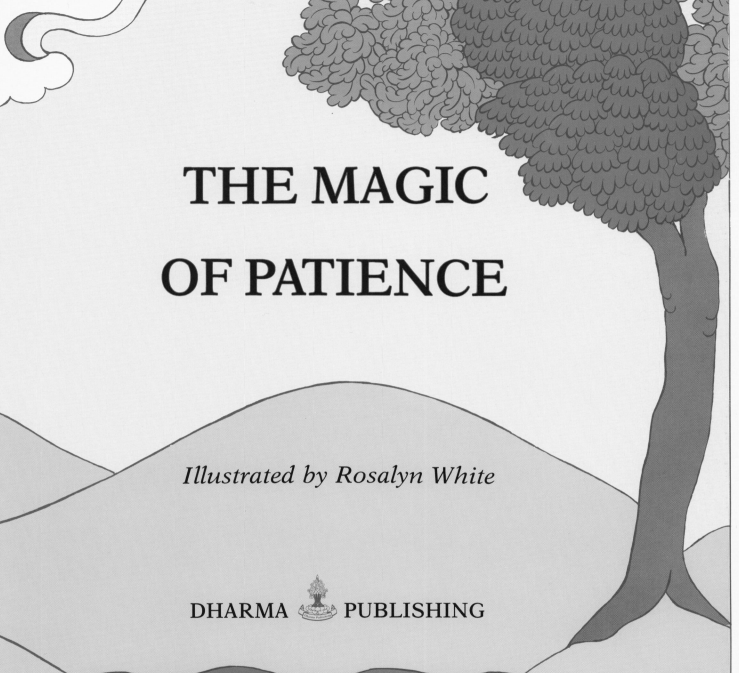

THE MAGIC
OF PATIENCE

Illustrated by Rosalyn White

DHARMA PUBLISHING

Dedicated to

All the World's Children

The Jataka Tales

The Jataka Tales celebrate the power of action motivated by compassion, love, wisdom, and kindness. They teach that all we think and do profoundly affects the quality of our lives. Selfish words and deeds bring suffering to us and to those around us while selfless action gives rise to goodness of such power that it spreads in ever-widening circles, uplifting all forms of life.

The Jataka Tales, first related by the Buddha over two thousand years ago, bring to light his many lifetimes of positive action practiced for the sake of the world. As an embodiment of great compassion, the Awakened One reappears in many forms, in many times and places to ease the suffering of living beings. Thus these stories are filled with heroes of all kinds, each demonstrating the power of compassion and wisdom to transform any situation.

While based on traditional accounts, the stories in the Jataka Tales Series have been adapted for the children of today. May these tales inspire the positive action that will sustain the heart of goodness and the light of wisdom for the future of the world.

Tarthang Tulku   *Founder, Dharma Publishing*

Once upon a time deep within a jungle there lived a Great Being in the form of a wild buffalo. On the outside he seemed stern and frightening, but on the inside his heart was gentle and kind. In this same jungle lived a mischievous monkey, who insulted and annoyed the buffalo every day.

When Buffalo was about to feed on the grass, Monkey would play a trick. "Try and eat! Try and eat! Even though I stand under your feet!"

When Buffalo went to bathe in the river, Monkey would play a different trick. "Don't slip and fall! Don't slip and fall! Even though you can't see at all!"

When Buffalo wished to take a nap, Monkey would play yet another trick. "Give me a ride! Give me a ride! Or my stick will beat your hide!"

But Buffalo patiently endured all the tricks. He never hurt the little monkey or even frightened him away, and continued to treat him as a friend.

One day a magical forest sprite caught sight of these monkey tricks, and became very angry. "O Great Buffalo, why do you put up with this foolish monkey? What could you be thinking? Are you afraid of him? Have you become his slave? Does he know some terrible secret about you that he threatens to tell? The strongest lions fear your wrath! And even elephants step out of your path! With those hooves of yours, you could crush him to bits! With those horns of yours, you could shred him in strips!"

"O Forest Sprite," Buffalo replied, "anger never leads to happiness. Monkey does me a great favor by giving me an opportunity to defeat my anger, to practice patience. By learning patience, I protect myself as well as others. How good I feel inside when I am patient. Anger does not upset my heart, and I do not have to hurt someone and feel sorry later."

But the forest sprite could not understand. "This rascal's tricks will only worsen if you don't wise up and teach him a lesson!"

"It is better to be patient, my friend, for this may awaken his inner feelings. Though Monkey is mischievous, like all creatures, he possesses a true heart."

The forest sprite was amazed, for he had not figured out how to handle a tease, even though he knew all manner of magic and spells. "Patience! What a magical charm! Could you teach me how to do it? Show me quickly! Show me now! For I want to know how to use it."

"To practice patience," replied Buffalo, "you need a real rascal to help you. It's no use practicing on gentle and kind creatures, for they require no patience. What you need is a good monkey. Would you like to use mine?"

"Monkey! That tease! If he tried his silly tricks on me, I'd show him some of mine!"

"My friend, you see how hard patience is to practice. But you must keep trying. For it is indeed a magic charm."

"I learned to be patient by thinking about Monkey. His teasing will surely get him in trouble. Sooner or later, he will play a trick on some quick-tempered creature, who will give him a bad scare or even a beating. Poor Monkey!

"Then I thought about how lonely he must be. None of the animals wants to be around him, and everyone wishes he would go away. Poor Monkey! Then I thought about how confused he is. He relies on bad qualities instead of good ones, turning all his cleverness and energy into mean tricks. And so I feel sorry for Monkey, and do not wish to cause him any more unhappiness."

"If I think it through, the way you do, then maybe I can learn patience too." And off flew the forest sprite to practice the wonderful new charm called patience.

Just then Monkey, who had been hiding in the trees listening to every word, came up to Buffalo. "I did not know I had such a good friend. I did not think I had any friends at all. How kind and strong you are to be patient with a monkey like me. Please forgive me for teasing and playing mean tricks, and let me be your friend."

If you think of all beings as your friends,
Tricks and teasing can do you no harm,
For your heart is protected by patience,
And patience works like a charm!

The Jataka Tales Series

Golden Foot

Heart of Gold

The Spade Sage

A Precious Life

Three Wise Birds

Courageous Captain

The Best of Friends

The King and the Goat

The Hunter and the Quail

The Parrot and the Fig Tree

The Proud Peacock and the Mallard

Great Gift and the Wish-Fulfilling Gem

A King, a Hunter, and a Golden Goose

The King and the Mangoes

The Value of Friends

The Rabbit in the Moon

The Power of a Promise

The Magic of Patience

The Fish King's Power of Truth

Library of Congress Cataloging in Publication Data

The Magic of patience.

   (Jataka tales series)
   Summary: Buffalo persists in being kind and patient
with the mischievous Monkey, despite all his annoying
tricks.
   1. Jataka stories, English. [1. Jataka stories]
I. White, Rosalyn, ill. II. Series.
BQ1462.E5M34   1989   294.3'823   88-33442
ISBN 0-89800-188-9
ISBN 0-89800-189-7 (pbk.)